21st
Century
Skills Library

COOL CAREERS

DENTAL HYGIENIST

BARBARA A. SOMERVILL

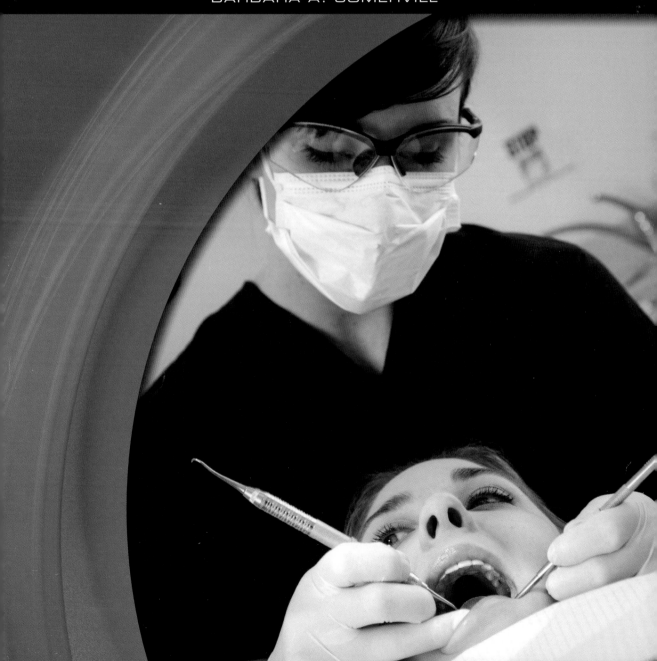

CHERRY LAKE Publishing

Published in the United States of America by
Cherry Lake Publishing, Ann Arbor, Michigan
www.cherrylakepublishing.com

Content Adviser
Sandra Nagel Beebe, RDH, PhD., Senior Lecturer Dental Hygiene/HCM Internship
Coordinator

Credits
Photos: Cover and page 1, ©iStockphoto.com/LeggNet; page 4, ©Lev Olkha/
Shutterstock, Inc.; page 6, ©Carme Balcells/Shutterstock, Inc.; page 9, ©siamionau
pavel/Shutterstock, Inc.; page 10, ©tadija/Shutterstock, Inc.; pages 12 and 16,
©Monkey Business Images/Shutterstock, Inc.; page 15, ©Lana K/Shutterstock,
Inc.; page 18, ©Robert Kneschke/Shutterstock, Inc.; page 21, ©iStockphoto.com/
dlewis33; page 22, ©Jim West/Alamy; page 24, ©iStockphoto.com/annedde;
page 25, ©Chamille White/Shutterstock, Inc.; page 27, ©GoGo Images Corporation/
Alamy; page 28, ©RubberBall/Alamy

Library of Congress Cataloging-in-Publication Data
Somervill, Barbara A.
  Dental hygienist/by Barbara A. Somervill.
    p. cm.—(Cool careers)
  Includes index.
  ISBN-13: 978-1-60279-938-7 (lib. bdg.)
  ISBN-10: 1-60279-938-5 (lib. bdg.)
  1. Dental hygienists—Vocational guidance—Juvenile literature.
  2. Teeth—Care and hygiene—Juvenile literature. I. Title. II. Series.
  RK60.5.S66 2010
  617.60023—dc22   2009053497

Cherry Lake Publishing would like to acknowledge
the work of The Partnership for 21st Century Skills.
Please visit *www.21stcenturyskills.org* for more information.

Printed in the United States of America
Corporate Graphics Inc.
July 2010
CLFA07

TABLE OF CONTENTS

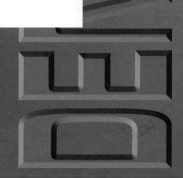

CHAPTER ONE
THE FIRST LINE OF DEFENSE

In a small town in Bolivia, a young girl squirms in a chair. It is the first time she has ever received dental care. The dental **hygienist** smiles at the girl and helps her relax. She gently

Dental hygienists work hard to help us stay healthy.

cleans the girl's teeth. Then she gives the girl a toothbrush, some toothpaste, and a package of floss. She teaches the girl how to use each item. Education is just as important as cleaning teeth for dental hygienists.

People gather at a senior citizen center to learn how they can reduce their chances of heart disease. They learn that the first step is to brush and floss regularly. A dental hygienist explains the close link between **periodontal** disease and heart disease in adults. Dental hygienists play an important role in overall healthcare.

21ST CENTURY CONTENT

Dental hygienists must honor their patients' privacy. It is against the law for health care workers to share any information about a patient without permission. The rules for respecting patients' privacy are set down in HIPAA, the Health Insurance Portability and Accountability Act of 1996.

Special Olympics Healthy Athletes worked with Miles of Smiles to provide on-the-spot dental care at the 2009 Winter

World Games. More than 300 dental professionals provided dental cleanings for more than 2,000 athletes. The Miles for Smiles program was started by dental hygienist Jennifer Via Clayton. Hygienists use their talents to help others. They have a commitment to better **oral** health for all citizens.

Dental hygienists do many things for their patients. They examine gums and measure the **pocket depths** around

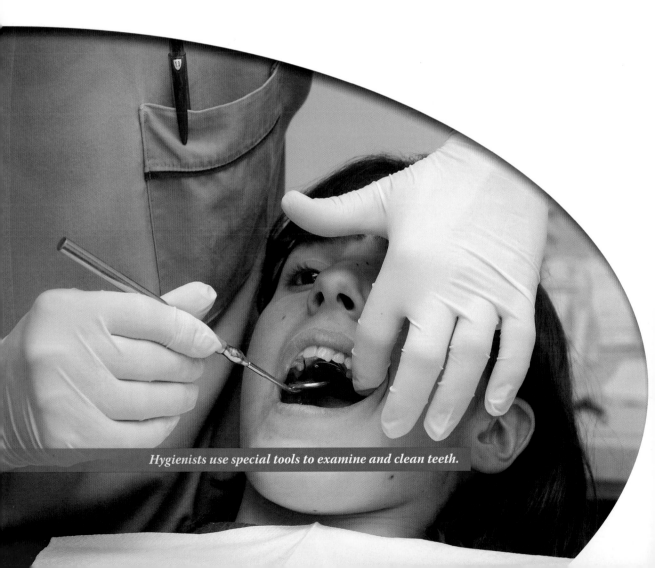

Hygienists use special tools to examine and clean teeth.

the teeth. They remove deposits from teeth. They also help prevent tooth decay by teaching about proper oral care. Hygienists usually begin a visit by asking if the patient is having any problems with his or her teeth. The patient's answers help the dentist and hygienist provide the best dental care.

The hygienist may take X-rays of the teeth. The dentist looks at the X-rays to see if there is any damage on the inside of the teeth. The hygienist examines the patient for chipped teeth, damaged fillings, discolored or swollen gums, and mouth sores. Then it is time to begin cleaning the teeth. The hygienist uses a hand mirror and **explorer** to find **plaque** and **calculus** on the teeth. Special tools are used to remove these harmful substances. This feels like poking or scraping on the teeth. Pocket depths are measured and recorded for each tooth. The hygienist then uses a powered toothbrush and a cleaning paste to leave teeth sparkling. After a good flossing, the patient is set for another 6 months.

Dental hygienists may give patients **fluoride** treatments or fluoride varnish to strengthen teeth. They sometimes place **sealants** in molars to prevent tooth decay. In some states, dental hygienists may place and carve filling materials. They can also help treat periodontal disease. Dental hygienists sometimes make mouth guards for athletes. These mouth guards help the athletes keep their teeth safe during sports.

In many states, a dentist must review a hygienist's work before the patient is finished. Dentists and hygienists work together closely. Dental hygienists must be good at working with patients, dentists, and other dental office workers.

21ST CENTURY CONTENT

Why do dental hygienists wear masks and gloves? The mouth is a breeding ground for **infection**. Dental hygienists must be careful not to spread these infections. Hepatitis, HIV, and tuberculosis can all be spread during dental care. That is why hygienists put on new latex gloves and masks for each patient. Tools are **sterilized** after every use. Safety glasses protect hygienists' eyes from spray. Disposable gowns or lab coats help them keep germs off their clothes.

Safety and cleanliness are important concerns for all health care professionals.

CHAPTER TWO
CLEAN TEETH, HEALTHY TEETH

Dental hygiene depends on the proper tools. The ancient Chinese made toothbrushes from the bristles of pigs. Ancient Egyptians, Romans, Chinese, Greeks, and Indians made rough toothpastes. Floss and toothpicks are as old as Egypt's pyramids. These instruments were not very

Brushing and flossing teeth at home is an important part of dental hygiene.

successful, though. It was very common for people to suffer from tooth pain. As recently as the early 1900s, the only solution for most dental problems was to remove teeth. Dental health care has come a long way since those days.

Today, dental care focuses on prevention. Preventing tooth decay and related problems is the main job of a dental hygienist.

LEARNING & INNOVATION SKILLS

Scientists are always developing better toothpastes, flosses, and toothbrushes. Today, we have whitening toothpastes to make brighter smiles. We have toothpastes to protect against gum disease, sensitivity, plaque build-up, and bad breath. Floss was once only available in a dentist's office. Now you can buy it at any drug store or supermarket. Toothbrushes include better-designed bristles for removing plaque. Some are even electric. Others include built-in scrapers to help clean your tongue while you brush. What are your ideas for improving dental care products?

In 1906, Dr. Alfred Civilion Fones of Bridgeport, Connecticut, had a bright idea. He trained Irene Newman to be the world's first dental hygienist. Newman took over preventive dental care and began cleaning patients' teeth. Fones' idea changed how dentists cared for their patients. Before then, dentists had never worried about preventing tooth decay. Instead, they just dealt with the problems caused by the decay.

Hygienists work closely with dentists to be sure each patient gets the best care.

Other dentists quickly saw how important dental hygienists could be. In 1913, Fones opened the Fones School of Dental Hygiene. It was the first school in the world to train dental hygienists.

Today, there are hygienists in nearly all dental offices. Besides working in offices, some hygienists also volunteer in clinics. Dental hygienists spend a lot of time talking to patients and dentists. This makes it an ideal job for people who like working with others.

 LIFE & CAREER SKILLS

The American Dental Hygienists' Association is an organization of dental hygienists and students in the United States and Canada. The group is made up of 375 local dental hygiene associations. The ADHA arranges continuing education for its members. It also publishes two magazines about dental hygiene: *Access* and *Journal of Dental Hygiene*. Its website (www.adha.org) offers information about the field of dental hygiene, school programs, and job benefits. The ADHA also offers scholarships for dental hygiene students.

The hours of most dental hygienists are flexible. Many work only 2 or 3 days a week. Some work for two or three different dentists. More than half work fewer than 35 hours a week.

Dental hygienists also work for schools, public health agencies, and the federal or state government. All branches of the military provide dental services. They will educate dental hygienists as part of military training.

Dental hygienists' pay depends on how much experience they have. It also depends on where they live and what type of dental practice they work in. A more experienced hygienist in a large city earns more than a recent graduate in a small town. Fifty percent of dental hygienists earn between $24 and $36 per hour. Newly hired hygienists may earn as little as $19 per hour. Some experienced hygienists earn as much as $42 per hour. The job market for dental hygienists is large and growing. Hygienists can work in cities, towns, and villages. They can move easily from one place to another because jobs are plentiful.

Dental hygiene is a growing career field.

CHAPTER THREE
BECOMING A DENTAL HYGIENIST

B ecoming a dental hygienist requires training, a **license**, and continuing education. Dental hygienists do

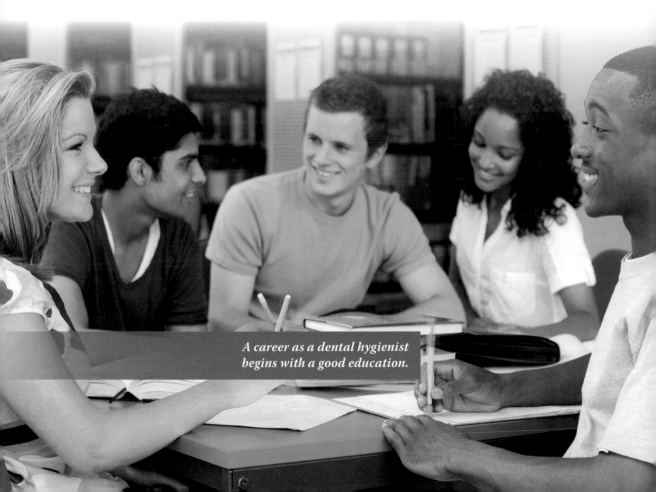

A career as a dental hygienist begins with a good education.

not need bachelor's degrees, but they do need special skills that can only be learned in school.

Students interested in dental health careers need a solid science background. They should study math, biology, chemistry, and English. It is also helpful to know a foreign language, especially Spanish. Dental hygiene programs require a high school diploma and college entrance test scores. Many schools require students to complete basic college courses in math, biology, and anatomy before entering a dental hygiene program. Classes in English, speech, psychology, and sociology are often required, too.

 LIFE & CAREER SKILLS

Dental hygienists never stop learning. They always need to learn about new instruments, improved materials, and better techniques for providing service to patients. They also need to keep up with new health concerns and changes in healthcare laws. Dental hygienists must take continuing education classes to keep their licenses.

There are more than 300 accredited dental hygiene programs in the United States and Canada. An accredited program is one that meets the requirements of the American Dental Association or the Canadian Dental Association. Community colleges, technical colleges, vocational schools, dental schools, and 4-year colleges or universities all offer dental hygiene programs. Most programs are designed for full-time students. The average cost of tuition and fees for a 2-year associate degree is about $30,000.

Dental hygiene classes include a lot of hands-on learning.

Slightly more than half of all basic dental hygiene programs are offered by junior or community colleges. Students can earn 2-year associate degrees at these schools. Some dental hygienists go on to earn bachelor's degrees, master's degrees, or doctorate degrees. An associate degree requires 86 credit hours of study. A bachelor's degree requires 122 credit hours. Three hours of class per week for a semester equals three credit hours. Space is limited in dental hygiene programs, so good grades are very important. Of four people who apply to a 2-year dental hygiene program, only one is accepted. One person out of every three who apply to a 4-year dental hygiene bachelor's program is accepted.

Course work includes both classes and clinical practice. Programs are very intense. A dental hygienist must spend more than 2,700 hours in classrooms or clinics to get an associate degree. This includes more than 650 hours working with patients under the supervision of a dental professional.

Students take courses in English, speech, and social studies. They also take many different science classes. This helps the students learn about the human body and how it is affected by food and drugs. Students also learn about radiology (taking and reading X-rays), pain control, and how to use dental materials.

Most dental programs require students to spend time working in public health facilities or community dental clinics. More than 6,000 new dental hygienists graduate each year. Licensed graduates have no problem finding jobs.

LIFE & CAREER SKILLS

A degree is a major accomplishment. It is not the only requirement for becoming a dental hygienist, though. Hygienists must pass the National Board of Dental Hygiene Examination to get a license. This is a long written test of dental hygiene knowledge. States also require hygienists to pass a clinical exam. This tests a hygienist's patient skills. Hygienists cannot use the letters RDH (Registered Dental Hygienist) after their names until they are licensed. No license means no job!

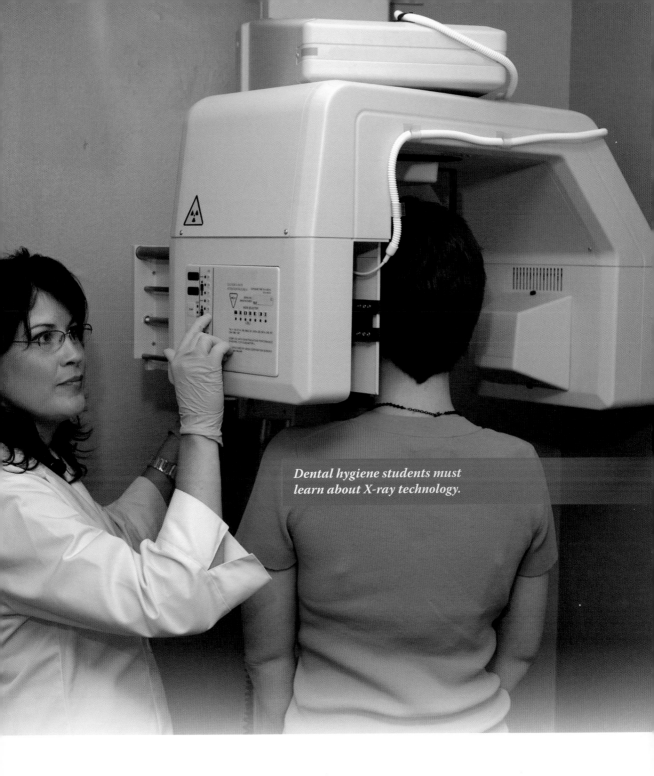

Dental hygiene students must learn about X-ray technology.

CHAPTER FOUR
A FUTURE IN DENTAL HYGIENE

The future of dental hygiene lies in helping all the people who aren't currently receiving dental care. Children

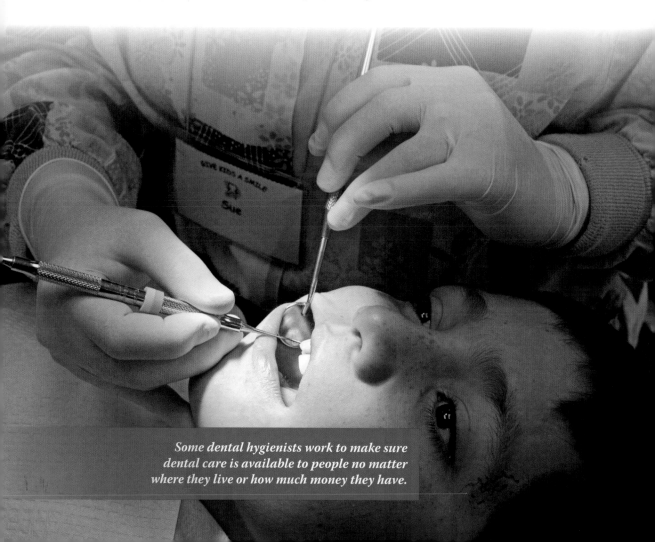

Some dental hygienists work to make sure dental care is available to people no matter where they live or how much money they have.

in low-income families have more cavities and more health problems related to tooth decay. This is because they lack access to proper dental care. There are also many other groups of people who are not receiving quality dental care. The American Dental Hygienists' Association has developed a plan to fix this problem.

LIFE & CAREER SKILLS

The American Dental Hygienists' Association and Johnson & Johnson started the Hygienist Hero program to honor dental hygienists who give back to their communities. One Hygienist Hero taught herself American Sign Language and volunteered her time to work with deaf patients. Another has spent 20 years volunteering to teach kindergarten children how to care for their teeth. Some Hygienist Heroes work with children. Others work with homeless people or the elderly. All of them promote quality oral healthcare. They represent the highest level of dental professionals.

Many dental hygienists volunteer their time and skills at schools, senior centers, and public health facilities. They sometimes work at free dental clinics in other countries. Many hygienists visit schools and daycare centers to teach children how to brush and floss their teeth.

Dental hygiene is an expanding field. Many hygienists today go on to earn bachelor's and master's degrees in

Some hygienists with advanced degrees research new ways to keep people's mouths healthy.

Teaching about proper dental care is a big part of a hygienist's job.

dental science. The American Dental Hygienists' Association is developing doctoral degree programs in dental hygiene. Hygienists with advanced degrees often work as teachers and researchers.

In recent years, the number of dentists graduating from dental school has declined by more than 20 percent. The number of dental hygiene graduates during the same time has increased by 20 percent. More than 174,000 dental hygienists currently practice in the United States. That number is expected to increase to 217,000 hygienists by 2016. This is an increase of 30 percent over present employment levels. About 97 percent of dental hygienists are women.

There are more hygienists than dentists. It is predicted that by 2020 there will be only 53 dentists for every 100,000 people in the United States. More dental hygienists will be needed to fill the gap made by the shortage of dentists.

LEARNING & INNOVATION SKILLS

Soon, there will not be enough dentists to serve the needs of the population. The American Dental Hygienists' Association has an idea that would help. They suggest creating a new job called an Advanced Dental Hygiene **Practitioner**. This new job would fall halfway between a dentist and a dental hygienist. An ADHP would be trained to do many of the same dental procedures that dentists do.

Oral healthcare is a big part of total health. Many signs of serious disease are first seen in the mouth. Quality dental care can help identify many of these diseases before they spread.

Maybe you would like to become a dental hygienist some day.

Gum disease can show if someone is at risk of heart disease, lung problems, diabetes, eating disorders, or osteoporosis. Poor dental health can be a sign of cancer or serious infections. There is a connection between a strong body and a healthy mouth. Still, nearly half of all Americans do not get regular dental check-ups.

Dental hygienists work hard to help protect our health. Every day, they battle against disease and poor hygiene. This work helps keep people happy and healthy. Does this sound like an exciting career to you? Maybe one day you will join the fight against poor dental health!

Dental hygienists have a bright career future!

SOME WELL-KNOWN DENTAL HYGIENISTS

Jennifer Via Clayton, RDH of Boise, Idaho, started the Special Smiles program in 2001 at the Idaho Special Olympics. The program has expanded since then. At the Special Olympics 2009 World Winter Games, Clayton arranged for a team of nearly 300 volunteers from around the world to screen and treat athletes at Miles for Smiles. Clayton has been recognized as a Hygienist Hero by the ADHA and Johnson & Johnson Healthcare Products.

Sandy Kemper, RDH of Seattle, Washington, works in the United States and Bolivia. She runs a non-profit organization called Smiles Forever. Kemper and her fellow hygienists provide dental hygiene for women and children in a homeless shelter in Bolivia. They also started a program to teach dental hygiene in Bolivia. The program teaches Bolivian women the skills they need to provide basic dental hygiene. Kemper also helped open a free dental clinic for the local Bolivian community.

Irene E. Newman (1875–1958) was the world's first dental hygienist. Newman worked with Dr. Alfred C. Fones, the Father of Dental Hygiene. Newman cleaned teeth and performed other preventive dental treatments on children as early as 1906. In 1917, Newman received the world's first dental hygiene license. She also became the first president of the first organization for dental hygienists, the Connecticut Dental Hygienists' Association.

Lynn Ramer, LDH is the 2009–2010 president of the American Dental Hygienists' Association. She has spent time educating preschool and kindergarten children on the importance of good oral health. Her dental office has participated in the Dentists Delivering Smiles program. She has also been active in the Doctors with a Heart program. This program provides services to people who cannot regularly afford dental care. Ramer received the Distinguished Hoosier Award from the Governor of Indiana.

GLOSSARY

calculus (KAL-kyuh-luhs) hard deposits on teeth

explorer (ek-SPLOR-ur) a dental tool used to check for tooth decay

fluoride (FLOOR-ide) a chemical compound containing fluorine that is used for hardening tooth enamel

hygiene (HYE-jeen) good health or cleanliness

hygienist (hye-JEHN-ist) a person who professionally cleans teeth

infection (in-FEK-shun) a bacterial or viral disease

license (LYE-suhnss) formal permission from the government to do something, such as working a job or driving a car

oral (OR-uhl) having to do with the mouth

periodontal (pehr-ee-oh-DON-tuhl) having to do with gums

plaque (PLAK) soft, sticky substance formed on tooth surfaces by bacteria

pocket depths (POK-it DEPTHS) measurements of how well gums are connected to teeth

practitioner (prak-TIH-SHUH-nur) a person who practices a profession

sealant (SEE-luhnt) a substance used for sealing the surfaces of molars

sterilized (STEHR-uh-lyzd) cleaned of infectious material

FOR MORE INFORMATION

BOOKS

Goulding, Sylvia. *Taking Care of Your Teeth*. Vero Beach, FL: Rourke Publishing, 2005.

Leake, Diyan. *Dentists*. Chicago: Heinemann Library, 2008.

Royston, Angela. *Tooth Decay*. Mankato, MN: Black Rabbit Books, 2008.

WEB SITES

ADHA—Important Facts About Dental Hygienists
www.adha.org/careerinfo/dhfacts.htm
Learn more about what dental hygienists do at the American Dental Hygienists' Association site.

Careers in the Field of Dentistry
www.ada.org/public/careers/team/hygienist.asp
Discover more about the field of dentistry and watch a video about dental hygiene careers.

Explore Health Careers
www.explorehealthcareers.org/en/Career.2.aspx
Find out more about the opportunities a health care career offers and watch a video about becoming a dental hygienist.

INDEX

ABOUT THE AUTHOR

Barbara Somervill is the author of more than 200 children's nonfiction books. She finds that investigating and writing about different careers is almost as good as starting a new career of her own. She readily admits that a visit to the dentist is not her favorite activity. After writing this book, however, she has a new respect for the ways that dental hygienists care for our health.